# Neil Armstrong

© **B. Jain Publishers (P) Ltd.** All rights reserved. No part of this book may be reproduced, stored in a retrieval system or transmitted, in any form or by any means, mechanical, photocopying, recording or otherwise, without any prior written permission of the publisher.

Published by Kuldeep Jain for B. Jain Publishers (P) Ltd., D-157, Sector 63, Noida - 201307, U.P
Registered office: 1921/10, Chuna Mandi, Paharganj, New Delhi-110055

Printed in India

# Contents

5   Who was Neil Armstrong?

6   Childhood and Early Life

11  Beginning of Career as a Pilot

18  Gemini Program

23  The Historic Mission of Apollo 11

35  Armstrong, the 'Cool' Astronaut

45  Death of Armstrong: The End of an Era

47  Legacy

50  Awards, Accolades and Achievements

56  Timeline

59  Activities

61  Glossary

# Who was Neil Armstrong?

Neil Armstrong was an American astronaut. He holds the distinction of being the first human to walk on the moon. When he was 20 years of age, Armstrong served in the Korean War, where he flew 78 combat missions. He received an Air Medal and two Gold Stars for the mission. In 1955, Armstrong graduated from Purdue University with a degree in aeronautical engineering. Armstrong is considered to be one of the greatest heroes of the space age, earning fame within the United States and the world over for being the first person to land a spacecraft on the moon!

# Childhood and Early Life

Armstrong, the man who created history in the unknown dark areas of space, was born on August 5, 1930 in Auglaize County near Wapakoneta, Ohio to Stephen Koenig Armstrong and Viola Louise Engel. His father worked as an auditor for the Ohio government, which meant that the family moved around quite a lot during Armstrong's formative years. In fact, the Armstrongs lived in a total of 20 towns for the first few years of junior Armstrong's life. From an early age, Armstrong demonstrated a deep passion for flying. When he was just two years old, his father took him to the Cleveland Air Races. On July 20, 1936, when he was five, he experienced his first airplane flight in Warren, Ohio, where he and his father took a ride in a Ford Trimotor airplane (also known as the 'Tin Goose').

From his very childhood, Armstrong was active in the Boy Scouts and obtained the rank of Eagle Scout. As a teenager, he began taking flying lessons and worked at the local airport and at other odd jobs in order to pay for it. At the age of 16, before he even had

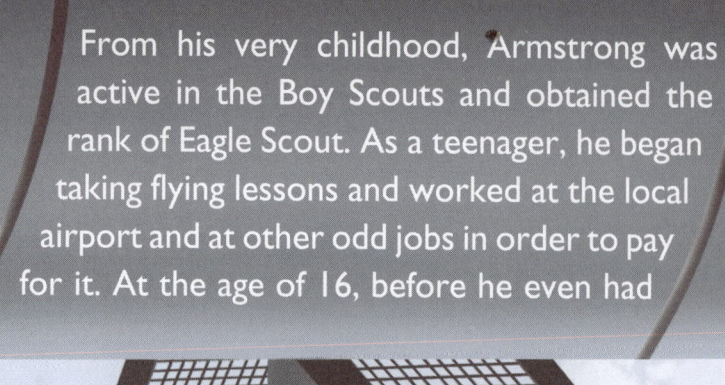

his driver's license, Armstrong earned his pilot's license and began his long, eventful journey down the path that would eventually take him into space. A serious pilot even at that age, Armstrong built a small wind tunnel (a tunnel through which air is forced at controlled speeds to study the effects of its flow) in the basement of his home. He also performed various experiments using the model planes he had made.

When he turned 17, Armstrong went off to study aeronautical engineering. Although he had been accepted to the Massachusetts Institute of Technology, he decided instead to go to Purdue University in West Lafayette, Indiana, in order to be closer to home. His college tuition was paid for under the Holloway Plan, where applicants committed to two years of study, followed by three years of service in the U.S. Navy, before completing the final two years of their degree programme.

# Beginning of Career as a Pilot

In 1949, in the month of January, when Armstrong was 18 years of age, he was called up for military service. He went off to the Naval Air Station in Pensacola, Florida, to begin his flight training, which lasted for almost 18 months. During this time, he qualified for carrier landing aboard the USS Cabot and USS Wright.

On August 16, 1950, two weeks after his 20th birthday, Armstrong was informed by an official letter that he was a fully qualified Naval Aviator. At 20, he was the youngest pilot in his squadron.

In June 1951, the carrier he had been assigned to—the USS Essex—set sail for Korea, where his unit (VF-51, an all-jet squadron) would act as a ground-attack squadron. In the course of the war, Armstrong flew 78 combat missions during the Korean War. It was a civil war from 1950 to 1953 between North and South Korea in which China fought on the Communist North Korean side and the United States fought to assist South Korea. Overall, Armstrong accumulated approximately 121 hours of combat experience. His plane was shot down once, but Armstrong managed to eject and was rescued without any serious injury.

For his service to his country, Armstrong received several commendations, including the Air Medal for his first 20 combat missions, a Gold Star for the next 20, and the Korean Service Medal and Engagement Star. Armstrong left the Navy at the age of 22, on August 23, 1952. Thereafter, he became a Lieutenant, Junior Grade, in the U.S. Naval Reserve. He remained in the reserve for eight years and then resigned his commission on October 21, 1960.

Armstrong returned to his studies at Purdue, after his service in Korea. In 1955, he was awarded a Bachelor of Science degree in Aeronautical Engineering and a Master of Science degree in Aerospace Engineering from the University of Southern California in 1970. Armstrong was also awarded Honorary doctorates by several universities later on in life.

It was also during his time at Purdue that Armstrong met Janet Elizabeth Shearon, the woman he married later. After completing a degree in aeronautical engineering in 1955, the two moved to Cleveland, Ohio, where Armstrong started working at the National Advisory Committee for Aeronautics' (NACA) Lewis Flight Propulsion Laboratory as a research test pilot. He married Janet on January 28, 1956, at the Congregational Church in Wilmette, Illinois.

After 18 months, the Armstrongs moved to Edwards Air Force Base in California, where Armstrong took up a job with the NACA's High-Speed Flight Station.

Here he became a skilled test pilot and flew the early models of such jet aircrafts as the F-100, F-101, F-102, F-104, F-5D, and B-47. He was also a pilot of the X-1B rocket plane, a later version of the first plane that broke through the sound barrier (the dragging effect of air on a plane as it approaches the speed of sound).

Armstrong was selected as a NACA pilot to fly the X-15 rocket-engine plane. He made seven flights in this plane, which was a kind of early model for future spacecraft. At one point, he set a record altitude of 207,500 feet and a speed of 3,989 miles per hour. Armstrong also received an invitation from the NASA American space-flight program, but until then he was little interested in becoming an astronaut. His heart lay in flying planes. Largely because of his experience with the X-15, he was selected as a pilot of the Dynasoar, an experimental craft that could leave the atmosphere, orbit earth, re-enter the atmosphere, and land like a conventional airplane.

It was also during this time that he met the legendary test pilot Chuck Yeager, and was involved in several incidents that went down in Andrew's AFB folklore.

# Gemini Program

In 1962, Armstrong finally made up his mind to become an astronaut and applied for NASA selection and training. In September the same year, he became America's first nonmilitary astronaut. He joined the NASA Astronaut Corps., which consisted of a group of nine astronauts who were popularly called by the press 'the New Nine'. These nine astronauts were selected for the Gemini and Apollo

programs. These programs, which were the successor to the Mercury Program—which sought to place an astronaut in orbit (popularized by the movie *The Right Stuff*)—were designed with the intent of conducting long-term space flights and a manned mission to the moon.

Armstrong's first mission to space took place four years later, on March 16, 1966, aboard a Titan II spacecraft, with Armstrong acting as command pilot and fellow astronaut David Scott as pilot. Known as Gemini 8, this mission was the most complex mission till date, involving a rendezvous and docking with an unmanned Agena Target Vehicle, and some extra-vehicular activity (EVA) being performed.

The docking procedure was a success, but due to mechanical failure, the mission had to be cut short. On September 12, 1966, Armstrong served as the Capsule Communicator (CAPCOM) for the Gemini 11 mission, remaining in communication with astronauts Pete Conrad and Dick Gordon as they conducted spacecraft rendezvous and EVA operations.

On April 5, 1967, just three-and-a-half months after the Apollo 1 fire took place, Deke Slayton—one of the Mercury Seven astronauts and NASA's first Chief of the

Astronaut Office—brought Armstrong and many other veterans of project Gemini together and told them that they would be flying the first lunar landing mission.

Over the next six months, Armstrong and the other astronauts began training for a possible trip to the moon. Armstrong was named as the backup commander for the Apollo 8 mission. On December 23, 1968, as Apollo 8 orbited the Moon, Slayton informed Armstrong that he would be commander for the Apollo 11 mission, joined by Edwin "Buzz" Aldrin as lunar module pilot and Michael Collins as command module pilot.

# The Historic Mission of Apollo 11

On July 16, 1969, Armstrong, with astronauts Michael Collins and Edwin "Buzz" Aldrin, lifted off from the Kennedy Space Center in Florida.

Thousands of people crowded the highways and beaches near the launch site to watch the Saturn V rocket ascend

into the sky. Millions more watched from home, and President Richard M. Nixon viewed the proceedings from the Oval Office at the White House.

The rocket entered the earth's orbit some twelve minutes later. After one-and-a-half orbits, the S-IVB third-stage engine pushed the spacecraft onto its trajectory toward the moon. After 30 minutes, the command/service module pair separated from this last remaining Saturn V stage, docked with the lunar module (a small spacecraft), and the combined spacecraft headed for the moon.

On July 19, Apollo 11 passed behind the moon and fired its service propulsion engine to enter the lunar orbit. On July 20, the lunar module Eagle separated from the command module Columbia, and the crew commenced their lunar descent. When Armstrong looked outside, he saw that the computer's landing target was in a boulder-strewn area, which he judged to be unsafe. As such, he

took over manual control of the lunar module, and the craft landed with only 25 seconds of fuel left!

Armstrong then radioed to Mission Control and announced their arrival saying, "Houston, Tranquility Base here. The Eagle has landed." Once the crew had gone through their checklist and depressurized the cabin, the Eagles' hatch was opened. At 10:56 p.m., Armstrong exited the lunar module and began walking down the ladder to the lunar surface first.

When he reached the bottom of the ladder, Armstrong said, "I'm going to step off the LEM now" (referring to the Lunar Excursion Module). He then turned and set his left boot on the surface of the moon on July 21, 1969, and spoke the famous words, "That's one small step for [a] man, one giant leap for mankind."

For about two-and-a-half hours, Armstrong and Aldrin collected samples and conducted experiments. They also took photographs, including those of their own footprints.

Returning on July 24, 1969, the Apollo 11 craft came down into the Pacific Ocean, west of Hawaii. The crew and the craft were picked up by the U.S.S. Hornet, and the three astronauts were put into quarantine for three weeks.

Before long, the three Apollo 11 astronauts were given a warm welcome home. Crowds lined the streets of New York City to cheer the famous heroes, who were honoured in a ticker-tape parade. Armstrong received many awards for his efforts, including the Medal of Freedom and the Congressional Space Medal Honour.

In addition, the Apollo 11 crew went on a 45-day tour around the world called the 'Giant Leap' tour. Armstrong also travelled to the Soviet Union to talk at the 13th annual conference of the International Committee on Space Research. While there, he met Valentina Tereshkova (the first female astronaut to go into space) and Premier Alexei Kosygin. He also received a tour of the Yuri Gagarin Cosmonaut Training Centre.

Shortly after the Apollo 11 mission, Armstrong announced that he did not intend to fly in space again.

Armstrong remained with NASA, serving as deputy associate administrator for aeronautics until 1971. After leaving NASA, he joined the faculty of the University of Cincinnati as a professor of aerospace engineering. He remained at the university for eight years. Staying active in his field, he served as the chairman of Computing Technologies for Aviation, Inc., from 1982 to 1992.

He also spent much of this time acting as a corporate spokesperson and serving on the board of directors of several companies.

During his post-Apollo years, Armstrong also served on two spaceflight accident investigations. The first took place in 1970, where he served as part of the panel that investigated the Apollo 13 mission, presented a detailed chronology of the mission, and made recommendations.

In 1986, President Ronald Reagan appointed him as vice-chairman of the Rogers Commission to investigate the space shuttle Challenger disaster of that year.

Even in his final years, Armstrong remained committed to space exploration. The press-shy astronaut returned to the spotlight in 2010, to express his concerns over changes made to the U.S. space program.

Helping out at a difficult time, Armstrong served as Vice Chairman of the Presidential Commission on the space shuttle Challenger accident in 1986. The commission investigated the explosion of the Challenger on January 28, 1986, which took the lives of its crew, including school teacher Christa McAuliffe.

# Armstrong, the 'Cool' Astronaut

Armstrong was a very humble hero despite his commendable achievements, which actually is a landmark in human history. Due to his immensely humble nature, he was fondly called the 'cool man' of NASA.

As a young man Neil Armstrong did many odd jobs, even one involving a walk among the dead. When he was 10 years old, Armstrong was paid US$ 1 to mow the cemetery in Wapakoneta, Ohio, the small town where he was born. It was one of many odd jobs the enterprising young Armstrong did around town, and eventually earned enough money to pay for US$ 9 per hour flying lessons. While other teens were learning how to drive a car, young Armstrong was getting into a cockpit to fly an aircraft! He fell in love with flying at an early age, and earned his pilot's license on his 16th birthday even before he received his driver's license!

Before he was a hero astronaut, he was a 'gofer'. Armstrong worked as a 'gofer' for pilots at the local airport. One day, he helped a pilot push his sleek Luscombe plane to the gas pumps, cleaned its windows and polished its gleaming surfaces, which earned him a ride and a flying lesson.

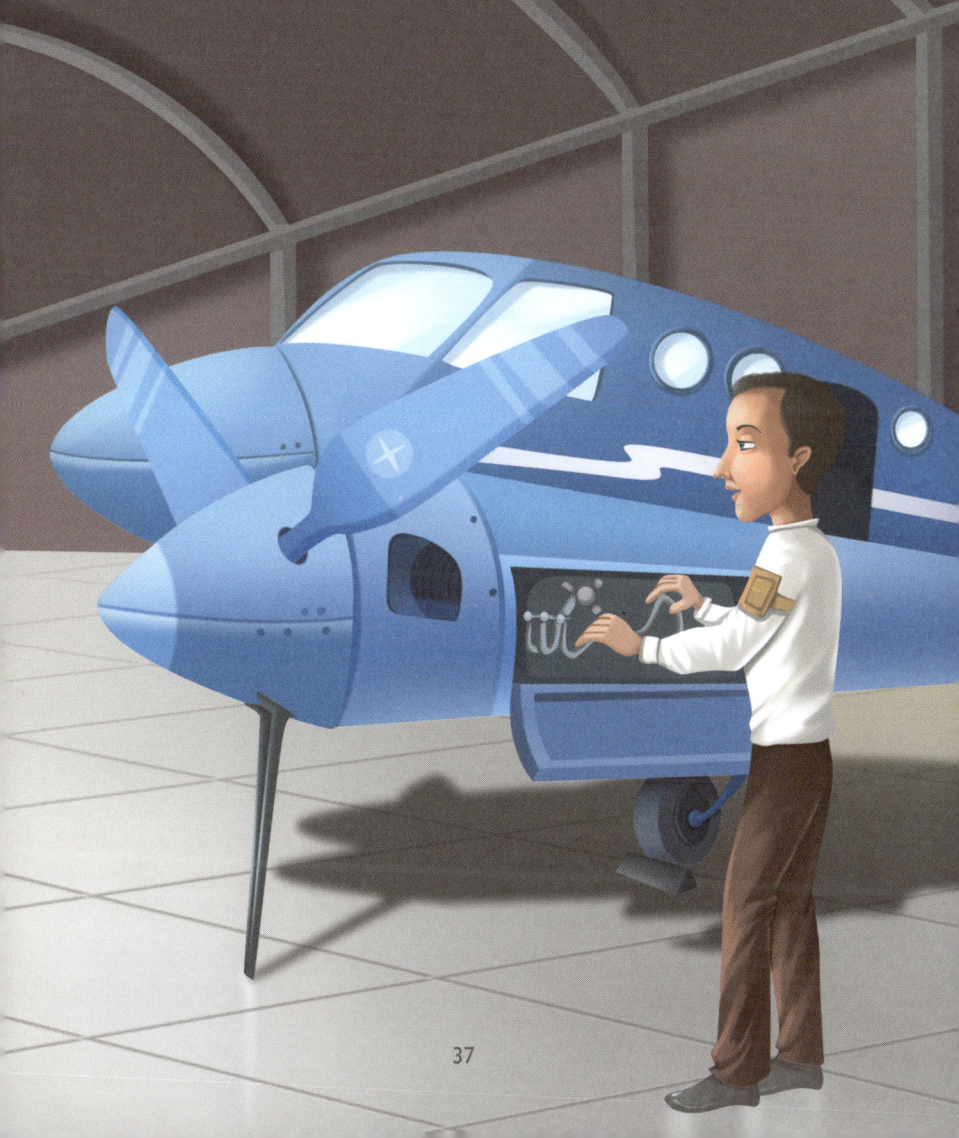

After graduating from college, Armstrong became a test pilot. He could fly over 200 different types of aircrafts from the dangerous rocket plane the X-15—which could reach a top speed of 4,000 miles per hour—to gliders, which he called sailplanes.

When the time came to choose the astronaut to first step onto the moon, Armstrong's well-deserved reputation for humility and perfectly honed flying skills won him this coveted opportunity.

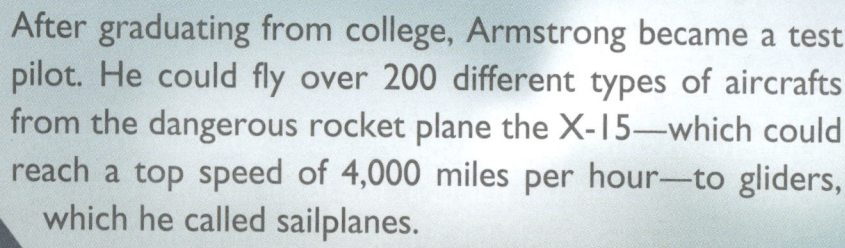

All his life, in whatever he did, Armstrong personified the essential qualities and core values of a superlative human being. His friends and work-mates remember him as a remarkable human being and pilot, who as a young man barely 20 years old, not only flew 78 combat missions over North Korea, but showed extraordinary levels of commitment, dedication, dependability, a thirst for knowledge, self-confidence, toughness, decisiveness, honesty, innovation, loyalty, positive attitude, self-respect, respect for others, integrity, self-reliance, prudence, judiciousness and much more.

One story that his biographer remembers is an event that happened when he was taking a flight over North Korea while on a dawn combat patrol in 1951. Passing over a ridge of low mountains in his F9F Panther jet, Armstrong saw laid out before him rows and rows of North Korean soldiers, unarmed, doing their daily calisthenics outside their field barracks. He could have mowed them down with machine-gun fire, but he chose to take his finger off the trigger and fly on. He later confided to his biographer, "It looked like they were having a rough enough time doing their morning exercises."

There was something too honorable in Armstrong for him to kill men who were in no position to defend themselves. Armstrong was quite adamant that he did not want this story in his biography. So, the masses came to know of it only after his death.

As for the first moon landing 18 years later, no human being could have handled the bright glare of international fame or the instant transformation into a historic and cultural icon better than Armstrong. It was in Armstrong's mild and modest personality to avoid publicity and keep to the real business of the engineering and piloting profession he had chosen. He was simply not the sort of man ever to seek what he felt was undeserved profit from his name or reputation.

In this highly competitive world today, many of us get uncomfortable when we are met with blocks in our lives and run away from them, rather than confronting the problem. Armstrong possessed a trait that others lacked, and it was this trait that made him and his actions stand out from others. The reason why Armstrong was able to endure through all the hardships life threw at him was because he met every obstacle head on with his never-failing bravery.

Armstrong never forgot to think of and thank the people who had helped him do what he had done. He was a person who valued privacy and rejected most opportunities to profit from his fame. In our world of greed and selfishness, pride takes over people's thoughts and actions. Armstrong could have chosen a popular, easy life but he chose to avoid the media. He could have made most of the opportunities that came as perks of fame but he chose to be treated like everybody else. He did not put himself above anyone else because of his success. Armstrong saw equality in all

men and believed that everybody deserved to be treated the same way irrespective of rank or status. He did not feel that he was more important than anybody else to be receiving so much attention. As he took his step on the moon, Armstrong said that he '... thought about all those 400,000 people that had given me the opportunity to make that step....''

Armstrong remained a humble and thankful person throughout his life, unmoved and unchanged by fame or praise. He always remembered the people who had

given him the opportunity to make the decisions he made. He repaid the support the people had given him by continuously contributing to the world with his good deeds. Armstrong was a kind of a person, who had a strong heart to resist temptations and to continue to be humble.

He had been a foremost member of the team that achieved humankind's first forays into deep space. He always emphasized the teamwork of the 400,000 Americans instrumental to Apollo's success. He had been at the top of that pyramid, but there had been nothing foreordained

in his becoming the commander of the first moon landing or becoming the first man out onto the lunar surface. As he always explained, it was mostly the luck of the draw, a series of contingent circumstances. Nevertheless, he had done what he had done, and he understood what great sacrifice, what commitment, and what extraordinary human creativity it had taken to get it done. He was immensely proud of the role he had played in the first moon landing, but he would not allow it to turn into a circus performance for him or a money-making machine.

# Death of Armstrong: The End of an Era

Photograph of Armstrong as a boy at his family memorial service in Indian Hill, Ohio near Cincinnati on August 31, 2012.

On August 7, 2012, Armstrong underwent a vascular bypass surgery to relieve blocked coronary arteries. Although he was reportedly recovering well, he developed complications in the hospital and died on August 25, in Cincinnati, Ohio. After his death, Armstrong was described, in a statement released by the White House, as 'among the greatest of American heroes—not just of his time, but of all time'. The statement further said that Armstrong had carried the aspirations of the US citizens and that he had delivered 'a moment of human achievement that will never be forgotten'.

On September 14 the same year, Armstrong's remains were scattered in the Atlantic Ocean during a burial-at-sea ceremony aboard the USS Philippine Sea.

Armstrong's colleague on the Apollo 11 mission, Aldrin said that he was 'deeply saddened by Armstrong's passing. I know I am joined by millions of others in mourning the passing of a true American hero and the best pilot I ever knew. I had truly hoped that on July 20, 2019, Neil, Mike and I would be standing together to commemorate the 50th Anniversary of our moon landing ... Regrettably, this is not to be.'

A tribute was held in Armstrong's honour on September 13 at Washington National Cathedral, whose Space Window depicts the Apollo 11 mission and holds a sliver of moon rock amid its stained-glass panels. The people who attended ceremony were Armstrong's Apollo 11 crew mates, Michael Collins and Buzz Aldrin; Eugene A. Cernan, the Apollo 17 mission commander and last man to walk on the moon; and former Senator and astronaut John Glenn, the first American to orbit the Earth.

# Legacy

Shortly after Armstrong's death, his family described him in a statement thus:

We are heartbroken to share the news that Neil Armstrong has passed away following complications resulting from cardiovascular procedures.

Neil was a loving husband, father, grandfather, brother, and friend.

Neil Armstrong was also a reluctant American hero who always believed he was just doing his job. He served his Nation proudly, as a navy fighter pilot, test pilot, and astronaut. He also found success back home in his native Ohio in business and academia, and became a community leader in Cincinnati.

He remained an advocate of aviation and exploration throughout his life and never lost his boyhood wonder of these pursuits.

As much as Neil cherished his privacy, he always appreciated the expressions of goodwill from people around the world and from all walks of life.

While we mourn the loss of a very good man, we also celebrate his remarkable life and hope that it serves as an example to young people around the world to work hard to make their dreams come true, to be willing to explore and push the limits, and to selflessly serve a cause greater than themselves.

For those who may ask what they can do to honour Neil, we have a simple request. Honour his example of service, accomplishment and modesty, and the next time you walk outside on a clear night and see the moon smiling down at you, think of Neil Armstrong and give him a wink.

News of Armstrong's death quickly spread around the world. President Obama was among those offering their condolences to his family and sharing their remembrances of the late space pioneer. 'Neil was among the greatest of American heroes—not just of his time, but of all time,' Obama was quoted in the *Los Angeles Times*.

# Awards, Accolades and Achievements

The achievement of Armstrong as the first man on the moon will remain unsurpassed in human history. For his remarkable dedication to his work, he was bestowed with many honours and awards, including the Presidential Medal of Freedom, the Congressional Space Medal of Honour, the Robert H. Goddard Memorial Trophy, the Sylvanus Thayer Award, the Collier Trophy from the National Aeronautics Association, and the Congressional Gold Medal. The lunar crater Armstrong, 31 mi (50 km) from the Apollo 11 landing site and asteroid 6469 Armstrong are named in his honour.

Armstrong was also inducted into the Aerospace Walk of Honour, the National Aviation Hall of Fame, and the United States Astronaut Hall of Fame. Armstrong and his Apollo 11 crew mates were the 1999 recipients of the Langley Gold Medal from the Smithsonian Institution.

Throughout the United States, there are more than a dozen elementary, middle and high schools named in his honour, and many places around the world have streets, buildings, schools, and other places named after Armstrong and Apollo.

In 1969, folk songwriter and singer John Stewart recorded 'Armstrong' a tribute to Armstrong and his first steps on the moon. Purdue University announced in October

2004 that its new engineering building would be named Neil Armstrong Hall of Engineering in his honour. In 1971, Armstrong was awarded the Sylvanus Thayer Award by the United States Military Academy at West Point for his service to the country. The Armstrong Air and Space Museum, in Armstrong's hometown of Wapakoneta, Ohio, and the airport in New

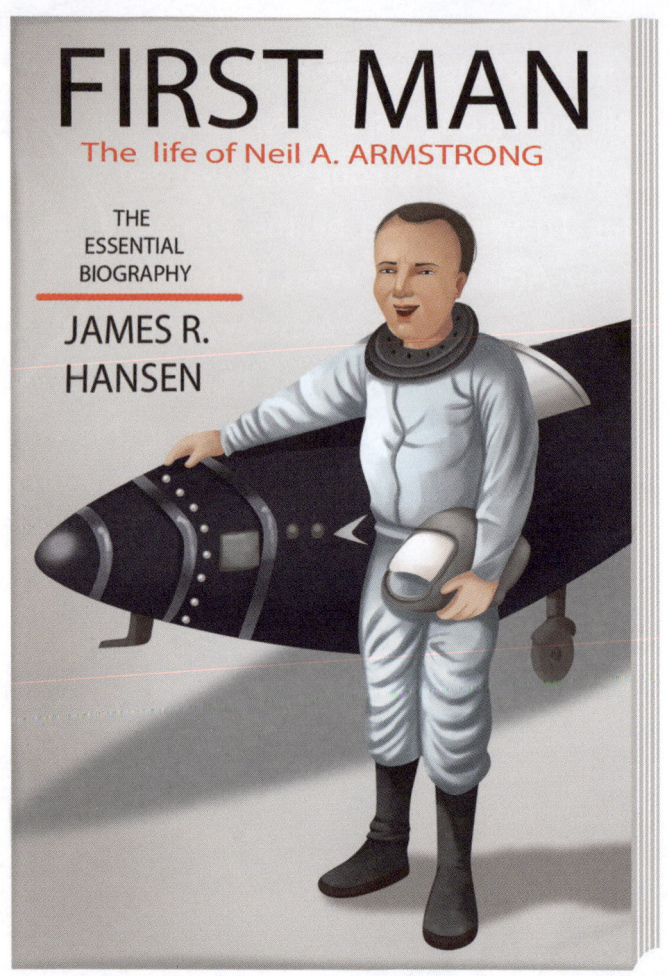

Knoxville, where he took his first flying lessons when he was 15, were named after him.

Michael Collins, President George W. Bush, Neil Armstrong, and Buzz Aldrin during celebrations of the 35th anniversary of the Apollo 11 flight, July 21, 2004.

Armstrong's authorized biography, *First Man: The Life of Neil A. Armstrong*, was published in 2005. For many years, Armstrong turned down biography offers from authors such as Stephen Ambrose and James A. Michener, but agreed to work with James R. Hansen after reading one of Hansen's other biographies.

In a 2010 Space Foundation survey, Armstrong was ranked #1 most popular space hero, and in 2013, Flying magazine ranked him #1 on its list of the 51 Heroes of Aviation.

The press often asked Armstrong for his views on the future of spaceflight. In 2005, Armstrong said that a manned mission to Mars will be easier than the lunar challenge of the 1960s, "I suspect that even though the various questions are difficult and many, they are not as difficult as those we faced when we started the Apollo [space program] in 1961."

In September 2012, the US Navy announced that the first Armstrong-class oceanographic research ship will be named RV Neil Armstrong. The ship, christened on March 28, 2014, and scheduled for entry into service in 2015, was designed to be a modern oceanographic research platform capable of supporting a wide range of oceanographic research activities conducted by academic groups.

- Armstrong was conferred with many prestigious awards including Presidential Medal of Freedom, Congressional Space Medal of Honor, Robert H. Goddard Memorial Trophy, Sylvanus Thayer Award and Collier Trophy from the National Aeronautics Association.

- He was also honoured with the Congressional Gold Medal, NASA Distinguished Service Medal, Langley Gold Medal, American Astronautical Society Flight Achievement Award and the John J. Montgomery Award.

- He was inducted in the Aerospace Walk of Honor and the United States Astronaut Hall of Fame.

- An asteroid in space and a lunar crater have been named after him. Many schools, institutions, streets, buildings, airports and public squares across the globe have been named after him.

- He received the 2013 General James E. Hill Lifetime Space Achievement Award from the Space Foundation.

# Timeline

- **1930** Birth of Neil Armstrong

    Neil Armstrong was born on August 5, 1930 in Ohio.

- **1946** Armstrong begins to fly

    Armstrong loved flying things from the time he was young. He earned his student pilot's license when he was just 16.

- **1947** Armstrong starts attending college

    Armstrong joined the US Navy. He also attended Purdue on scholarship, where he studied aeronautical engineering.

- **1949** Armstrong goes to war

    Armstrong was called into action with the U.S. Navy to fight in the Korean War. When the war came to an end, he returned to college.

- **1952** Armstrong joins NASA

    After returning from the war, Armstrong started working with an organization that would later be called NASA.

- **1956** Armstrong gets married

Armstrong tied the knot with his girlfriend, Janet Shearon, in 1956.

■ **1962** Armstrong joins the astronaut program

In 1962, Armstrong shifted his family to Texas so he could work with the astronaut program.

■ **1966** Armstrong goes to space

Armstrong, along with his flight partner David Scott, was launched into space to dock with the Gemini Agena vehicle. The dock was successful, but the mission had to be cut short.

■ **1969** Armstrong's mission to the moon

Armstrong, along with two other astronauts, landed on the moon. Armstrong drove the lunar module.

■ **1969** Armstrong gets awarded for his efforts

Armstrong and his partners in flight received many awards for the success of their moon mission. Some of the awards included the Medal of Freedom and the Congressional Space Medal of Honor.

■ **1971** Armstrong leaves NASA

## Timeline

Neil left NASA to become a professor in Ohio, at the University of Cincinnati.

- **1986 Armstrong becomes the investigator**

    Armstrong helped investigate the failed space mission, the Challenger, in 1986. The Challenger blew up after launch, killing its crew.

- **2006 Armstrong on 60 Minutes**

    Armstrong enjoyed his privacy, and he stayed out of the public eye for years. In 2006, he gave a TV interview on 60 Minutes, and later that year his biography was released.

- **2010 Armstrong speaks out**

    In 2010, President Barack Obama made cuts to the space program, a move against which Armstrong publically spoke out.

- **2012 Armstrong dies**

    Armstrong died at the age of 82, after complications from heart surgery.

## Class Discussion

What is your idea about space? Discuss with your teacher and classmates. Also discuss about things that you know exist in space.

## Group Activity

Divide yourselves in groups and collect pictures from the internet on the famous astronaut Neil Armstrong, his moon walk and Apollo 11. Make a collage by sticking those pictures. You may cut the sheet in the shape of a rocket. See the picture given below.

## Questions

1. When and where was Armstrong born?
2. Who were his parents?
3. What was Armstrong fond of from an early age?
4. Do you think his father had a lot of contribution behind this? Why?
5. What did Armstrong go to study at the age of 17?
6. Which university did he join and why?
7. Why did he go to Naval Air Station in Pensacola, Florida at the age of 18?

## Activities

8. What did he qualify for at the age of 20?
9. In which year did Armstrong join the Korean War?
10. In the year 1955, what degree did Armstrong get?
11. What did the term 'new nine' mean at NASA?
12. Who were Armstrong's companions in Apollo 11?
13. When did Armstrong and Aldrin walk on the moon finally?
14. How much time did they spend researching on the moon?
15. When did they return from the moon?
16. Where did the spacecraft land?
17. What was the 'giant leap'?
18. What did Armstrong do after retiring from NASA?
19. Why was Armstrong called the 'cool man' at NASA?
20. Mention three qualities of Armstrong as a human being.
21. How did this remarkable astronaut die?
22. Mention some of the honours bestowed on Armstrong.

# Glossary

**accumulate:** to gather

**achievements:** something done successfully with effort

**aeronautical engineering:** a field of engineering concerned with the development of aircraft and spacecraft

**announce:** to give information about transport in a station or airport through a public address system

**auditor:** a person who conducts an audit

**calisthenics:** gymnastic exercises to achieve bodily fitness and grace

**commendations:** an award given for very good performance in something

**committed:** pledged or bound to someone or something

**decisiveness:** the ability to make decisions

**dedication:** the quality of being committed

**demonstrate:** to show clearly the existence of something by giving evidence

**depressurize:** release the pressure of the gas inside

**derivatives:** something which is based on another source

## Glossary

**docking:** an enclosed area of water in a port for the loading, unloading, and repair of ships

**enterprising:** showing initiative in some activity

**explosion:** a violent shattering or blowing apart of something due to a bomb blast

**gleaming:** to shine brightly

**gofer:** a person who runs errands, especially on a film set or in an office

**honorable:** bringing or deserving honour

**honorary:** conferred as an honour, without the usual requirements

**Immensely:** extremely

**incidents:** something happening; an occurrence

**innovation:** to make something new

**integrity:** to be honest and have strong moral principles

**investigation:** the formal or systematic examination of something or on someone

**judiciousness:** showing, or doing things with good judgement

**legendary:** as described in legends

**lunar orbit:** the orbit of an object around the moon

# Glossary

**manned:** having a human crew

**oceanographic research:** to study the oceans

**passion:** very strong and uncontrollable emotion

**pioneer:** a person who is among the first to explore

**proceedings:** a series of activities involving a set procedure

**propulsion:** to drive or push forwards

**prudence:** the quality of being cautious

**publicity:** attention given to someone or something by the media

**quarantine:** a period or place of isolation in which people or animals with contagious disease are placed

**recommendation:** a proposal as to the best course of action

**reluctant:** hesitant

**rendezvous:** a meeting at an agreed time and place

**self-reliance:** to rely on one's own powers

**selflessly:** concerned more with the needs and wishes of others than with one's own

**spacecraft:** a vehicle used for travelling in space

## Glossary

**squadron:** an operational unit in an air force consisting of two or more flights of aircraft and the personnel needed to fly them

**trajectory:** a flight path that a moving object follows through space as a function of time; the object might be a projectile or a satellite

**undeserved:** not warranted

**unmanned:** a place without staff

**unsurpassed:** better or greater than any other

**vascular:** relating to vessel or vessels